THE
TOMATO
COOKBOOK

Varieties text written by
Joy Larkcom

THE
TOMATO
COOKBOOK

EDITED BY
NICOLA HILL

Mitchell Beazley

First published in Great Britain in 1994
by Mitchell Beazley
an imprint of Reed Consumer Books Limited
Michelin House, 81 Fulham Road, London SW3 6RB
and Auckland, Melbourne, Singapore and Toronto

Copyright © 1994 Reed International Books Limited

ISBN 1 85732 411 0

A CIP catalogue record for this book is available from
the British Library

Printed in Singapore

Acknowledgements

Art Director: Jacqui Small
Art Editors: Meryl James & Sue Michniewicz
Commissioning Editor: Nicola Hill
Editors: Isobel Holland & Jo Lethaby
Production Controller: Sasha Judelson
Jacket Photographer: Nick Carman
Photographer: Alan Newnham
Home Economist: Jennie Shapter
Stylist: Jane McLeish
Illustrator: Roger Kent/Garden Studio

Notes

Both metric and imperial measurements have been
given in all recipes. Use one set of measurements only
and not a mixture of both.

Standard level spoon measurements are used in all
recipes.
1 tablespoon = one 15 ml spoon
1 teaspoon = one 5 ml spoon

Eggs should be size 3 unless otherwise stated.

Milk should be full fat unless otherwise stated.

Ovens should be preheated to the specified temperature
– if using a fan assisted oven, follow the manufacturer's
instructions for adjusting the time and the temperature.

To skin tomatoes, make a small cross in the top of each
tomato. Drop them into a bowl of boiling water and
leave for 2-3 minutes. Remove with a slotted spoon
and allow to cool. The skin should now come off easily
but if the tomatoes are slightly under-ripe they may
need a little longer in the boiling water before the skins
can be easily removed.

No two people agree on what constitutes a well-flavoured tomato, but perhaps 'tart sweetness' is as good a description as any. Some people prefer the acidic element, others the sweetness but it is the subtle balance of the two in one fruit which seems to create outstanding flavour. For the best tomatoes marry this with the texture of the flesh and juiciness. Most people love a 'meaty' tomato and juiciness – as long as the juice is flavour-some and not just 'watery'. What cooks and the discerning public abhor is the 'taste of nothing' characteristic of so many bought tomatoes.

Flavour is influenced by many factors, the variety being one of the most important. Unfortunately many of today's commercial varieties are bred to travel well or to stand up to mechanical harvesting; flavour has been a casualty.

Secondly, a crucial factor in retaining flavour is, when the tomatoes are picked. Within reason, the longer the fruit is left on the plant the better, and the sooner it is eaten once ripe, the better the flavour. The home gardener has the edge every time, as commercial tomatoes are often picked when green, plunged into cold storage and later ripened in warming rooms. This process eliminates most of the flavour.

Flavour is also affected by how tomatoes are grown. Ironically, tomatoes taste better if the plants are to some degree maltreated – a little underwatered and a little underfed. (Bad gardeners can grow very tasty tomatoes!) Even within one variety, flavour can vary during the season, from truss to truss, with the temperature, with the quality of light, and whether they are grown indoors or out.

Most varieties taste best when the skin colour is fully developed and the flesh is firm. Curiously, good flavour seems to be associated with some of the green-shouldered varieties, which never fully turn red.

Tomato Types and Their Uses Apart from the standard round red tomato, there are several distinct types, some being better suited to one purpose than others. While most tomatoes are red-skinned when mature, yellow forms exist in almost all types. Less common however, are tomatoes with pink, orange, and near white skins, while a few rare types remain green-skinned even when mature.

Varieties * = in UK & USA cats.

BEEFSTEAK TYPE
* Burpee's Big Boy
As its name implies, a very large beefsteak tomato, with fruits often well over 500 g (*1 lb*) in weight. Introduced in the 1940s, it has always been noted for its productivity and good flavour. Individual fruits are bright red, very smooth, firm, well-shaped, with thick walls and meaty flesh. Multipurpose. An indeterminate hybrid variety.

Dombello
A large-fruited beefsteak, with fruits averaging 175-275 g (*6-9 oz*) in weight. Fruits are very deep red at maturity, with some greenback on the shoulders. They are exceptionally meaty and juicy, having very little central core. Flavour is good. Muiltipurpose; they are excellent sliced and grilled. A semi-indeterminate hybrid.

* Dona
A beefsteak tomato with slightly flattened, very glossy fruits, averaging 150-175 g (*5-6 oz*) each. Well-flavoured, with an excellent acid/sweet ratio and good meaty texture. Excellent general purpose tomato; ideal for slicing in salads and for using in sandwiches. A semi-indeterminate hybrid.

* Golden Boy
Very large, well-flavoured, nicely rounded, firm fleshy fruits, often 5-7 cm (*2-3 in*) in diameter and weighing up to 500 g (*1 lb*). Wonderful deep golden-orange skin colour, making it eye catching in salads. General purpose, high quality fruit. A semi-indeterminate hybrid.

Golden Boy

MARMANDE TYPE
* Marmande/Supermarmande
The classic, misshapen, irregularly ribbed French tomato. 'Supermarmande' is an improved form of the original 'Marmande' type. Its outstanding flavour and texture more than compensate for its ugliness, though plenty of sunshine is necessary to develop the full flavour. Large, firm fruits are recommended both for use raw in salads and for cooking. Fairly early maturing, with semi-indeterminate habit.

Supermarmande

CHERRY TYPE
* Gardener's Delight
Surely one of the most popular of modern tomatoes? Cherry-sized, thin-skinned, bright red fruits with exceptionally sweet flavour. Juicy 'bite sized' fruits are about 2.5 cm (*1 in*) in diameter. Best used fresh in salads, but can be frozen whole. Very vigorous, tall growing indeterminate plants, notable for their healthiness and abundant cropping.

* Sweet 100
Very similar to Gardener's Delight in fruit and habit,

though the shiny, bright red fruits are a little smaller. Nicely balanced flavour: whether you prefer Gardener's Delight or Sweet 100 is purely a question of personal taste.

Sweet 100

Sweet Million
A variety which may supercede Sweet 100 in the USA as a salad tomato. The sweet-flavoured, medium-sized 'cherry' fruits weigh 15-20 g (½-¾ oz) each. Plants fruit over a long season and keep well after picking. An indeterminate hybrid, noted for its disease resistance and for its productivity. One plant may produce over 500 fruits!

Sweet Chelsea
Large cherry tomatoes, averaging 4 cm (1¾ in) in diameter, and weighing 20-25 g (¾-1 oz).

Good, exceptionally sweet flavour. Essentially used fresh in salads. Becoming a popular gardeners' variety, as plants have wide range of disesase resistance, and crop early and abundantly. Fruits have good resistance to splitting and cracking late in the season. Hybrid, medium height, indeterminate plant, but side branches will set fruit if left untrimmed.

Sweet Chelsea

Tumbler
A British bred variety suited for cool climates. Well-flavoured, smallish fruits about 3 cm (1½ in) in diameter. Primarily a salad variety. A determinate bush hybrid, ideally suited to growing in pots and hanging baskets as the side shoots cascade over the edges making it a decorative plant.

Phyra
A small-fruited gardeners' variety, notable for the technicolour effects of the grape-sized fruits as they ripen, crowding the plant with green, yellow, orange and red fruit simultaneously. The tiny fruits are slightly pointed, with an acidic flavour. Because of this, they are recommended as a salad garnish. A determinate, bushy hybrid about 30 cm (12 in) tall, suited to growing in containers. However in favourable conditions this plant can become quite rampant and sprawling.

* Sungold
The tomato everyone loves - the golden counterpart for Gardener's Delight. Cherry size, thin-skinned fruits with exceptionally high sugar content. This accounts for the very sweet flavour which has been described as 'tropical' and 'winey'. Very vigorous, tall growing, heavily cropping, healthy plants, typical of modern hybrids. Suitable for growing indoors or out even in cool climates.

GOLDEN PEAR SHAPED
* Yellow Pear
Daintily waisted fruits, 2.5-5 cm (1-2 in) long and generally about

7

2.5 cm (*1 in*) diameter 'across the beam'. Pretty in salads and very appealing to children. Reports on its flavour vary from 'wonderful' to 'slightly acid' and 'lemony' to 'charming, pleasant and mild' perhaps reflecting a wider response than most to growing conditions. Undeniably it can be bland. Ideally used in salads for its decorative qualities, but can be lightly cooked. Indeterminate plants.

Yellow Pear

PASTE, CANNING TYPE
*Roma VF/Roma
The classic, long, almost conical Italian tomato bred especially for canning. The heavy fleshy fruits are almost seedless.

Roma

Relatively lacking in flavour, but has excellent qualities for making soups, sauces, purées, pastes and juices, and also suitable for barbecuing. Vigorous, essentially bush habit, but can be grown as an upright, given some support. Plants are very prolific in reasonable conditions.

Britain's Breakfast
A British-bred tomato, with fairly cylindrical, boxy fruits with a little pixie point at the top. Dense flesh and small seed cavity, like Italian paste tomatoes, and suited for use in purées and soups and in cooked dishes. Especially recommended for freezing. Has a distinct sweet

flavour and is equally good as a sliced salad tomato. An indeterminate variety, that doesn't normally grow very tall. Individual trusses can produce so many fruits that thinning is necessary! Over 100 fruits have been known to grow on one truss.

*San Marzano
The standard Neapolitan 'paste' tomato, with long, blocky, deep red fruits characterised by a tiny 'pinnacle' at the top end. The true San Marzano should be able to stand upright on its square shoulders. Fruits notable for their high proportion of solid flesh and very small seed cavity, so ideal for making pastes and purées as far less boiling is necessary than with juicier varieties. Recommended also for bottling, canning and drying. Mild flavour with satisfactory sweet/acid balance. Moderately vigorous indeterminate plants.

STANDARD ROUND RED TOMATO
Shirley
A commercial European variety, producing heavy crops of firm, round, medium-sized fruits of about 5 cm (*2 in*) diameter. Well-flavoured, with a good sugar/acid balance. Suitable for

salads and for cooking. A fairly compact indeterminate hybrid, noted for its good disease resistance and early cropping, and recommended mainly for growing in cold and slightly heated greenhouses in a cool climate.

Shirley

Ailsa Craig
An old British favourite with a devoted following. Nicely shaped, round, mid-red, high quality fruits with particularly fine flavour, described as essentially sweet with a touch of acid. However, many strains have been developed and some have a noticeably better flavour than others. Essentially a salad tomato for fresh use. Indeterminate, heavily cropping plants, suitable for growing outside and in greenhouses.

* Pixie
Very popular, bright red, medium-sized tomato of 4 cm (*1³/₄ in*) diameter. Fruits well flavoured and meaty. Good general purpose tomato. A hybrid with a very compact bush habit, making it ideal for container growing. Notable for its earliness, hardiness, productivity and fast ripening fruit. The improved Pixie hybrid has excellent disease resistance.

Alicante
An old established European variety, noted for medium-sized, high quality, smooth, fairly sweet and well-flavoured fruit. Acceptable for using either fresh

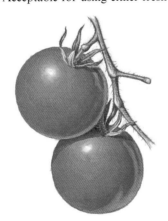

Alicante

or for cooking. Popular with gardeners because of its earliness, reliability, and versatility. Grown outdoors and under cover. Tall indeterminate variety.

Counter
A popular commercially grown European hybrid. Smooth, firm, round tomatoes with good texture. Flavour noticeably sweet but very pleasantly balanced with acidity. Quite fragrant. Used in salads and for cooking. Moderately tall indeterminate habit, with good disease resistance. Mainly a greenhouse variety.

Moneymaker
A well-established European variety, producing uniform, round, red tomatoes, up to 5 cm (*2 in*) in diameter. Very popular with amateur gardeners on account of its reliability. Its detractors say it is flavourless, but its advocates deny this. (The former are probably correct.) General purpose use. Indeterminate habit.

Nepal
Introduced to the USA by a Johnny's Seeds customer and reputedly originating from Nepal, the round, red fruits vary

from moderate size in cool climates to near beefsteak size in good growing conditions. Flesh is firm and flavour outstanding. The flavour is retained even after plants are exposed to low end-of-season temperatures. Excellent.in salads and for cooking. Moderately vigorous indeterminate habit.

Celebrity
An American hybrid, notable for its firm, well-flavoured globe to slightly flattened fruits which average about 200 g (*7 ozs*) in weight but can be much heavier. The tomatoes are rated highly for their colour, texture, flavour and resistance to cracking. General purpose use. Very popular with gardeners on account of its vigour, disease resistance and general productivity. A determinate bush variety – but it may benefit from some support to control its natural vigour.

STRIPED TOMATO
Tigerella
Popular, round to plum shaped, medium-sized tomatoes up to 5 cm (*2 in*) in diameter. A pretty appearance as the skin is marked with red and orange stripes. Good, distinct flavour. Mainly used in salads for its novelty appeal. Indeterminate

habit, early ripening and heavy yielding. In Europe grown outdoors and under cover.

Tigerella

YELLOW TOMATOES
Golden Sunrise
Round, smooth, very even, large fruits about 5 cm (*2 in*) diameter, notable for the yellow gold skin colour. Normally a good, sweet flavour. Essentially a salad tomato but can be cooked. A semi-indeterminate variety, which can be grown as a bush.

Golden Boy
A popular American tomato. Large, firm textured fruits, often weighing as much as 500 g (*1 lb*). Fruits are deep yellow orange both inside and out, with notable flavour. Good for gen-

eral purpose use. Vigorous, indeterminate hybrid.

Lemon Boy
An American introduction, notable for its 'shocking yellow' skin colour and lemony flesh. Fruits are smooth, deep globular in shape, and average 175-200 g (*6-7 oz*) in weight. The flavour is mild, but the fruits are very eye catching in salads. An early cropping, high yielding indeterminate hybrid, with good disease resistance.

Yellow currant
Bred by the British family seed firm, Robinsons, these tiny

Yellow Currant

grape-sized tomatoes are a yellow orange when ripe. Thin-skinned, juicy, and mild-flavoured, they are tailor made for use as a decorative salad garnish. Clusters can be picked whole. Indeterminate, rampant plants, which can be grown as cordons, or, if they are pruned especially hard, as bushes in large containers.

PINK TOMATOES
Ponderosa Pink
Popular American variety, with very large fruits, often weighing 750 g (*1½ lb*) each. Fruits are solid with firm, meaty flesh and small seed cavity. The skin colour is an unusual purplish-pink. Very sweet, mild flavour; excellent used sliced in salads and sandwiches and can be cooked. Late maturing indeterminate variety.

* Oxheart Giant Oxheart/Grosso Gigante Cuor de Bue
An old Italian variety, producing large, sometimes enormous heart-shaped tomatoes, often weighing well over 500 g (*1 lb*). Fruits are noted for their very thick walls and dense, solid flesh, they have little internal cavity and very few seeds. Their colour is an attractive pink. Excellent flavour and

texture. Good for use in salads and fillings for sandwiches, for grilling and frying and also for stuffing. An indeterminate, early cropping variety.

STORAGE TOMATO
Long Keeper
A unique tomato, originally sent to the American seed company Burpee by one of its customers, on account of its ability to store well for long periods after picking. The ripe fruits have an attractive golden orange skin colour, with medium red flesh. They have a high acid content and a reasonable flavour, which is certainly superior to any out of season commercial tomatoes.

Long Keeper

For storage pick unblemished or partially ripe fruit before they have been touched by frost, and store indoors so they ripen naturally. They will usually keep from 6-12 weeks, and sometimes longer. Indeterminate plant habit.

Striped Cavern

STUFFING TOMATO
Striped Cavern
Very boxy fruit, often 5 cm (*2 in*) deep with exceptionally thick walls. The inside can be scooped out to make a wonderful cavity for stuffing. Especially when immature, the skin appears lightly striped. Unexciting flavour: definitely for use as the messenger, not the message. Vigorous, indeterminate plants.

ITALIAN TOMATO SOUP

Serves 4-6

2 tablespoons olive oil
2 garlic cloves, halved
1 onion, chopped
750 g (*1½ lb*) tomatoes, skinned,
seeded and chopped
1 litre (*1¾ pints*) beef stock
1 tablespoon tomato purée
2 tablespoons uncooked long-grain rice
1 tablespoon chopped fresh basil
salt and freshly ground black pepper
basil leaves, to garnish

Heat the oil in a large saucepan, add the garlic and fry until golden brown. Remove and discard the garlic. Add the onion and tomatoes to the garlic-flavoured oil and fry for 2-3 minutes, stirring frequently.

Add the beef stock, tomato purée, rice and chopped basil. Simmer over a low heat, for about 15 minutes. Season with salt and pepper to taste.

Transfer to a warmed soup tureen and garnish with basil leaves. Serve with freshly grated Parmesan and French or garlic bread, if liked.

TOMATO & COURGETTE SOUP

Serves 4

3 tablespoons olive oil
1 garlic clove, crushed
1 kg (*2 lb*) tomatoes, skinned,
seeded and chopped
2 tablespoons tomato purée
1 tablespoon chopped fresh basil
750 ml (*1¾ pints*) chicken stock
2 courgettes, trimmed and coarsely shredded
salt and freshly ground black pepper

TO GARNISH:

4 ice cubes
3 tablespoons natural yogurt
basil leaves

Heat the oil in a saucepan, add the garlic, tomatoes and tomato purée and cook over a gentle heat for 10 minutes. Stir in the basil and stock with seasoning to taste. Bring to the boil, lower the heat and simmer for 5 minutes. Purée the soup in a liquidizer or food processor until fairly smooth. Leave to cool. Stir the courgettes into the soup; cover and chill for 4 hours, or overnight.

Just before serving place an ice cube in each of four chilled bowls. Pour in the soup, add a swirl of yogurt and garnish with basil leaves.

Illustrated opposite

GAZPACHO

Serves 6

500 g (*1 lb*) beefsteak tomatoes, skinned,
seeded and chopped
2 garlic cloves, chopped
3 tablespoons tomato purée
3 tablespoons olive oil
2 tablespoons red wine vinegar
600 ml (*1 pint*) water
½ teaspoon sugar
1 cucumber, halved
salt and freshly ground black pepper

TO SERVE:

1 small onion, chopped,
or 6 spring onions, chopped
croûtons (optional)

Place the tomatoes in a liquidizer or food processor with the garlic, tomato purée, olive oil, vinegar, half the water and sugar. Add salt and pepper to taste. Skin and roughly chop one cucumber half and add to the processor. Blend at maximum speed for 30 seconds, or until smooth. Stir in the remaining water. Refrigerate the soup for at least 2 hours.

Just before serving, dice the remaining cucumber and sprinkle it over the chilled soup with the chopped onion and croûtons, if using, or serve separately in small bowls.

Illustrated on pages 2-3

TOMATO & ROSEMARY SOUP

Serves 4

2 tablespoons olive oil
1 large onion, chopped
300 g (*10 oz*) potatoes, peeled and diced
625 g (*1¼ lb*) ripe tomatoes, roughly chopped
grated rind and juice of ½ lemon
750 ml (*1¼ pints*) chicken or vegetable stock
2 rosemary sprigs
salt and freshly ground black pepper

Heat the olive oil in a saucepan. Add the onion and fry over a moderate heat for 5 minutes, then add the potatoes and stir until well coated in oil. Cook gently for 5 minutes, stirring occasionally.

Add the tomatoes, lemon rind and juice, stock and rosemary sprigs, with salt and pepper to taste. Bring to the boil, lower the heat and simmer the soup for 15-20 minutes.

Purée the soup in a liquidizer or food processor. Press through a sieve to remove the tomato seeds and rosemary. Return the soup to the clean pan, adjust the seasoning to taste and reheat. Serve in individual heated bowls.

PEPPER & TOMATO SOUP

Serves 4

2 tablespoons sunflower oil
1 onion, finely chopped
2 green peppers, cored, seeded and chopped
1 garlic clove, crushed
500 g (*1 lb*) tomatoes, skinned,
seeded and chopped
1 tablespoon tomato purée
750 ml (*1¼ pints*) vegetable stock
1 teaspoon dried basil
salt and freshly ground black pepper

TO GARNISH:

2 tablespoons natural yogurt or soured cream
chopped fresh parsley

Heat the oil in a saucepan and sauté the onion until soft. Add the green peppers and cook for 2 minutes. Stir in the garlic, tomatoes, tomato purée, vegetable stock and basil, with salt and pepper to taste.

Bring the soup to the boil, cover and simmer for 30 minutes. Allow to cool slightly. Purée in a liquidizer or food processor, or rub through a sieve. Return the soup to the rinsed pan and reheat gently. Pour into heated soup bowls. Swirl a little of the yogurt or soured cream into each bowl and garnish with chopped parsley.

TOMATO & CRAB SOUP

Serves 4-6

50 g (*2 oz*) butter
2 onions, sliced
1 garlic clove, crushed
750 g (*1½ lb*) tomatoes, skinned,
seeded and chopped
1 bouquet garni
150 ml (*¼ pint*) dry white wine
750 ml (*1¼ pints*) fish stock
2 teaspoons grated lemon rind
300 g (*10 oz*) cooked crab meat
150 ml (*¼ pint*) double cream
salt and freshly ground white pepper

Melt the butter in a large saucepan. Add the onions and garlic and cook over a moderate heat until softened. Add the tomatoes, bouquet garni, wine, stock and lemon rind with half the crab meat. Stir in salt and pepper to taste. Bring to the boil, lower the heat, cover and simmer for 20 minutes.

Remove and discard the bouquet garni from the soup. Allow to cool slightly, then purée in a blender or food processor. Alternatively, press the soup through a fine sieve into the clean pan. Add the remaining crab meat and stir in the cream. Reheat but do not boil. Serve the soup hot with crusty French bread.

CHERRY TOMATO CUPS

Makes 50

**50 cherry tomatoes, a mixture of
red and yellow
175 g (*6 oz*) full-fat soft cheese
a little milk
175 g (*6 oz*) Brussels pâté
salt and freshly ground black pepper
parsley or dill sprigs, to garnish**

Cut the tops off the tomatoes and slice small pieces off the bases, if necessary, so that they will stand level. Using a teaspoon, scoop out the seeds; sprinkle the insides with a little salt and pepper.

Put the cheese into a bowl and beat well until smooth, adding a little milk if needed to make a piping consistency. Using a piping bag fitted with a shell nozzle, pipe the cheese into half the tomatoes; fill the remainder with pâté.

Garnish each tomato with a tiny sprig of parsley or dill, arrange on plates or trays and serve as hors d'oeuvres or as part of a buffet.

BURGHUL & TOMATO SALAD

Serves 4

**125 g (*4 oz*) burghul (cracked wheat)
500 g (*1 lb*) tomatoes, chopped
2 garlic cloves, crushed
2 onions, chopped
4 parsley sprigs, chopped
a few lemon balm leaves, finely chopped
2 tablespoons chopped fresh mint**
DRESSING:
**3 tablespoons lemon juice
6 tablespoons olive oil
1 teaspoon salt
pinch of white pepper**

Put the burghul in a bowl with water to cover. Soak for 45 minutes. Pour into a sieve lined with muslin or a clean tea towel, drain and then squeeze the cloth to extract as much liquid as possible from the burghul. Tip the burghul into a bowl. Add the tomatoes, garlic, onions and herbs. Mix lightly.

To make the dressing, combine the lemon juice, olive oil, salt and white pepper in a screw-top jar. Close the lid tightly and shake well. Pour the dressing over the salad and toss lightly. Set aside for at least 30 minutes to allow the flavours to blend. Serve at room temperature.

Illustrated opposite

TOMATOES WITH HORSERADISH SAUCE

Serves 4

500 g (*1 lb*) yellow currant or
cherry tomatoes
75 ml (*3 fl oz*) mayonnaise
2 tablespoons soured cream
2 tablespoons natural yogurt
2 teaspoons lemon juice
3 tablespoons horseradish sauce,
or 1-2 tablespoons grated horseradish
1½ tablespoons chopped fresh dill
1 dill sprig, to garnish

Pile the tomatoes in a pyramid on a flat dish. In a bowl combine the mayonnaise with the soured cream and yogurt, then stir in the lemon juice, horseradish and dill.

Spoon the horseradish sauce over the tomatoes just before serving. Garnish with the dill sprig.

CASHEW NUT & TOMATO SALAD

Serves 4

2 crisp dessert apples, peeled,
cored and roughly chopped
2 teaspoons lemon juice
50 g (*2 oz*) salted cashew nuts, chopped
4 plum tomatoes, sliced
lettuce leaves, to serve
1 tablespoon chopped fresh dill, to garnish

DRESSING:

1 tablespoon white wine vinegar
2 tablespoons sunflower oil
1 garlic clove, crushed
1 teaspoon wholegrain mustard
¼ teaspoon sugar
¼ teaspoon freshly ground black pepper

Put the chopped apples into a bowl and stir in the lemon juice, cashew nuts and tomatoes.

To make the dressing, combine all the ingredients in a screw-top jar. Close the lid tightly and shake well. Add the dressing to the tomato mixture and toss gently to coat all the ingredients.

Serve the salad in a bowl lined with lettuce leaves and garnish with chopped dill.

GREEN TOMATO & PASTA SALAD

Serves 4-6

500 g (*1 lb*) cooked pasta twists
1 kg (*2 lb*) large green tomatoes
2 tablespoons olive oil
6 garlic cloves, thickly sliced
1 tablespoon white wine vinegar
salt and freshly ground black pepper

Bring a large saucepan of lightly salted water to the boil. Add the pasta twists and cook until just tender. Drain, rinse under cold water and drain again. Transfer to a salad bowl.

Dice the tomatoes, removing as much seed pulp as possible. Heat the oil in a large frying pan, add the garlic and cook until golden. Stir in the tomatoes, cover the pan, and cook for 6-8 minutes over a low heat.

Stir the vinegar into the tomato mixture, with salt and pepper to taste. Add to the cooked pasta and toss lightly. Serve the salad cold or at room temperature.

TOMATOES WITH YOGURT & BASIL

Serves 4

750 g (*1½ lb*) tomatoes, skinned,
seeded and coarsely chopped
40 g (*1½ oz*) butter
200 ml (*7 fl oz*) natural yogurt
2 teaspoons chopped fresh basil
25 g (*1 oz*) pine nuts, toasted
salt and freshly ground black pepper
wholemeal toast triangles,
or slices of pitta bread, to garnish

Drain away any excess juice from the tomatoes by leaving them on a sloping board or in a colander for 10 minutes.

Melt the butter in a frying pan and cook the tomatoes gently for a few minutes, until just softened but not mushy. Remove the pan from the heat. Add salt and pepper to taste.

Beat the yogurt in a bowl until smooth, then stir into the tomatoes. Stir in the chopped basil, pour into a shallow serving dish and scatter the pine nuts over the top. Garnish with wholemeal toast triangles or with sliced pitta bread.

Serve immediately, or keep warm for a short time, but do not attempt to reheat after adding the yogurt. This dish should be served warm rather than hot.

PIQUANT TOMATO SALAD

Serves 4

2 plum tomatoes, quartered
2 firm round tomatoes, quartered
8 cherry tomatoes, halved
1 stick celery, sliced
1 red onion, thinly sliced
1 teaspoon cumin seeds
2 anchovy fillets, chopped

DRESSING:

4 teaspoons Dijon mustard
2 tablespoons white or red wine vinegar
75 ml (*3 fl oz*) olive oil
salt and freshly ground black pepper

To make the dressing, place the mustard in a bowl and stir in the vinegar. Season lightly with salt and plenty of pepper and whisk in the olive oil until the mixture is well blended.

Place the tomatoes in a salad bowl with the celery, onion, cumin seeds and anchovy fillets. Add the dressing and toss until all the ingredients are well mixed. Serve at once.

Illustrated on front jacket

TOMATO & FETA CHEESE SALAD

Serves 4

375 g (*12 oz*) beefsteak tomatoes, thinly sliced
1 red onion, thinly sliced
2 teaspoons chopped fresh oregano
125 g (*4 oz*) feta cheese, crumbled
4-6 tablespoons olive oil
salt and freshly ground black pepper

Arrange the tomato and onion slices on a serving plate. Sprinkle with the chopped oregano. Add the crumbled feta, with salt and pepper to taste.

Spoon the olive oil evenly over the top of the salad. Leave to stand at room temperature for 20 minutes to allow the flavours to mingle. Serve immediately.

Illustrated opposite

MIXED BARBECUED VEGETABLES

Serves 6-8

2 red onions
2 yellow peppers
2 green peppers
1 large aubergine
about 200 ml (*7 fl oz*) olive oil
2 garlic cloves, crushed
2 tablespoons chopped fresh parsley
8 plum tomatoes, halved
3 firm courgettes, halved lengthways
12 large firm mushrooms, trimmed
salt and freshly ground black pepper

Remove the outer skin from the onions, leaving the point intact. Cut each onion in half horizontally. Trim the stalk end of each pepper neatly. Cut the aubergine in half lengthways. Score the flesh, without cutting through the skin and sprinkle generously with salt. Leave to drain upside down on a wire rack for 30 minutes.

Brush the cut surface of the onion with olive oil and place cut-side down on a barbecue rack over hot coals. Brush the peppers with olive oil and place on the barbecue grill; once the skin is charred, turn them over. Continue to turn the peppers until the skin is completely charred, eventually standing them upright. Transfer to a plate.

Once they have cooled enough to handle, peel the peppers and cut them into strips, discarding the seeds. Put the strips into a bowl and add 4 tablespoons of the olive oil with salt and pepper to taste. Stir in the garlic and the parsley. As soon as the cut surfaces of the onions are charred, turn them over, making sure that they do not collapse, and move them to the edge of the barbecue grill. When the onions are charred all over and tender, cut them into chunks, discarding any parts that are very black. Add the onion to the peppers, stirring in a little extra oil.

Rinse the aubergine halves and pat them dry with kitchen paper. Brush the cut surfaces with olive oil and place cut-side down on the barbecue grill. Cook for 10-15 minutes, turning once during cooking. (The aubergine is cooked when the centre flesh is creamy and tender – it will become bitter if over-cooked.) Meanwhile, brush the tomatoes, courgettes and mushrooms with olive oil and cook for 8-10 minutes, turning during cooking.

When the mushrooms, courgettes, tomatoes and aubergines are cooked, transfer them to a shallow serving dish, and serve with the cold onions and peppers.

CELERIAC & TOMATOES WITH LEMON SAUCE

Serves 4

15 g (*½ oz*) butter
1 celeriac, coarsely chopped
150 ml (*¼ pint*) vegetable stock
4 tablespoons lemon juice
375 g (*12 oz*) tomatoes, cut into wedges
pinch of dried basil
1 egg yolk
2 tablespoons double cream
salt and freshly ground black pepper
basil sprigs, to garnish

Melt the butter in a large saucepan, add the celeriac and cook for 4-5 minutes. Add the stock and lemon juice and cook over a low heat for 5 minutes. Stir in the tomatoes and basil with salt and pepper to taste, taking care not to break up the tomatoes. Cook over a low heat, for about 7-10 minutes, or until the celeriac is tender.

Beat the egg yolk with the cream in a cup. Remove the vegetables from the heat and add the egg and cream mixture, stirring constantly. Transfer to a warmed serving dish, garnish with the basil and serve.

FRIED TOMATOES WITH CREAM

Serves 4

8 rashers rindless streaky bacon
2-3 large green or very firm red tomatoes, about 250 g (*8 oz*) each
50 g (*2 oz*) plain flour
grated nutmeg
a little butter (optional)
175 ml (*6 fl oz*) single cream
salt and freshly ground black pepper
chopped fresh parsley, to garnish

Gently fry bacon in a large frying pan until crisp. Remove with a slotted spoon; leave to drain on kitchen paper. Cut each tomato into eight slices, 1 cm (*½ inch*) thick, discarding the stem end and base. Season flour well with salt, pepper and nutmeg. Spread out on a plate, add tomato slices and coat on all sides.

Fry half the tomatoes in the rendered bacon fat over a moderately high heat until lightly browned. Turn once, adding a little butter if necessary to prevent sticking. Gently remove tomatoes and place on a serving plate; keep warm. Cook the remaining tomatoes.

Pour the cream into the pan, bring to the boil, scraping the bottom to incorporate the brown bits. Pour sauce over the tomatoes, garnish with the parsley. Arrange bacon rashers in a criss-cross pattern on the tomatoes and serve.

ITALIAN STUFFED TOMATOES

Serves 4

8 large round or 4 marmande tomatoes
1 tablespoon sunflower oil
1 garlic clove, crushed
1 large onion, finely chopped
2 sticks celery, finely chopped
125 g (*4 oz*) lean rindless bacon, finely chopped
50 g (*2 oz*) long-grain white rice, cooked
2 tablespoons sweetcorn kernels
1 teaspoon dried oregano or marjoram
2 tablespoons chopped fresh parsley
25 g (*1 oz*) grated Parmesan cheese
salt and freshly ground black pepper

Slice the tops off the tomatoes and reserve. Scoop out the insides and reserve. Heat the oil in a saucepan, add the garlic, onion, celery, bacon and tomato pulp and cook gently for about 5 minutes. Remove from the heat, mix in the rice, sweetcorn and herbs with salt and pepper to taste.

Fill tomatoes with bacon mixture, piling it up, and place in a lightly greased ovenproof dish. Sprinkle with Parmesan, replace tomato lids and cover. Bake in a preheated oven, 180°C (*350°F*), Gas Mark 4, for about 20-25 minutes until the tomatoes are cooked. Uncover for the last 5 minutes. Serve hot or cold.

Illustrated on page 1

TOMATO & VEGETABLE KEBABS

Serves 2-4

2 courgettes, sliced
24 yellow or red cherry tomatoes,
or a mixture of both
1 onion, cut into 8 wedges
8 shiitake mushrooms
MARINADE:
1 tablespoon soy sauce
2 tablespoons olive oil
1 teaspoon wholegrain mustard
salt and freshly ground black pepper

Mix the marinade ingredients together. Bring a saucepan of water to the boil. Add the courgette slices and blanch for 1 minute. Drain well.

Thread the cherry tomatoes, courgette slices, onion wedges and mushrooms on to four long or eight short skewers and brush with the marinade. Leave the kebabs to marinate for 30 minutes. Cook under a preheated grill or on a barbecue for about 5-10 minutes, turning from time to time. Serve immediately.

Illustrated opposite

SAUTEED CHERRY TOMATOES

Serves 4

50 g (*2 oz*) butter or margarine
1 large onion, sliced into rings
1 teaspoon dried basil
500 g (*1 lb*) cherry tomatoes
1 teaspoon sugar
salt and freshly ground black pepper
chopped fresh parsley, to garnish

Melt the butter or margarine in a frying pan. Add the onion and basil and sauté until softened. Add the tomatoes and sprinkle with sugar, salt and pepper. Cook over a moderate heat, stirring gently, for 3-4 minutes or just until the skins begin to split.

Spoon into a serving dish and sprinkle with chopped parsley. Serve hot.

OKRA WITH TOMATOES

Serves 4

75 g (*3 oz*) ghee, or 50 g (*2 oz*) butter
and 2 tablespoons sunflower oil
4 green cardamom pods, split open
1 small onion, thinly sliced
500 g (*1 lb*) okra, trimmed and sliced in chunks
500 g (*1 lb*) tomatoes, skinned and quartered
1 teaspoon garam masala
2 tablespoons chopped fresh coriander leaves
salt and freshly ground black pepper

Melt the ghee or butter and oil in a saucepan. Add the cardamoms. Fry these for a few seconds, then add the onion and a little salt and pepper. Cook until soft but not browned.

Add the okra and tomatoes to the pan and cook for 8-10 minutes, stirring the vegetables frequently. The okra should be tender – avoid overcooking them or they will become slimy and unpleasant in texture.

As soon as the vegetables are cooked, sprinkle on the garam masala and chopped coriander. Serve immediately as a vegetable dish or as an accompaniment to curries.

CAULIFLOWER & TOMATO SOUFFLE

Serves 4

½ cauliflower, divided into florets
40 g (*1½ oz*) butter
25 g (*1 oz*) fresh white breadcrumbs
250 g (*8 oz*) tomatoes, skinned and sliced
a few basil or tarragon leaves
75 g (*3 oz*) mature Cheddar cheese, grated
25 g (*1 oz*) plain flour
150 ml (*¼ pint*) milk
3 eggs, separated
salt and freshly ground black pepper

Cook cauliflower in salted boiling water until just tender. Drain, cool. Butter the inside of a 1.8 litre (*3 pint*) soufflé dish with 15 g (*½ oz*) of the butter, sprinkle dish with breadcrumbs. Place cauliflower and tomatoes in dish, season, sprinkle with herbs and half the cheese.

Melt remaining butter in a small saucepan. Stir in the flour, cook for 30 seconds. Add milk gradually, stirring until the sauce boils and thickens. Remove from heat. When cool, beat the egg yolks and add to sauce with 25 g (*1 oz*) of the remaining cheese. Season to taste.

Whisk egg whites and fold into sauce. Pour over the vegetables. Sprinkle with remaining cheese. Bake in a preheated oven, 190°C (*375°F*), Gas Mark 5, for 25-30 minutes or until risen and golden brown. Serve at once.

NUT-STUFFED TOMATOES

Serves 4

4 marmande tomatoes
salt

STUFFING:

3 tablespoons sunflower oil
125 g (*4 oz*) button mushrooms, finely chopped
125 g (*4 oz*) cooked brown rice
50 g (*2 oz*) Brazil nuts, coarsely chopped
45 g (*1½ oz*) currants
2 teaspoons chopped fresh basil,
or 1 teaspoon dried
freshly ground black pepper

TO GARNISH:

75 ml (*3 fl oz*) soured cream
watercress sprigs

Cut the tomatoes in half, scoop out the pulp and discard. Sprinkle the shells with salt and place in a baking dish. To prepare the stuffing, heat the oil in a small pan and gently fry the mushrooms for 5 minutes. Stir in the cooked rice, nuts, currants and basil. Add a little salt and plenty of pepper. Spoon the stuffing into the tomato halves.

Cover the dish with foil and bake in a preheated oven, 180°C (*350°F*), Gas Mark 4, for 25-30 minutes. Remove from the oven, top each stuffed tomato with a little soured cream and garnish with watercress. Serve piping hot.

COURGETTES NEAPOLITAN

Serves 4

1 tablespoon olive oil
1 small onion, chopped
1 garlic clove, chopped
500 g (*1 lb*) tomatoes, skinned,
seeded and chopped
750 g (*1½ lb*) courgettes, cut into
1 cm (*½ inch*) slices
2 tablespoons plain flour
25 g (*1 oz*) butter
250 g (*8 oz*) mozzarella cheese, grated
25 g (*1 oz*) Parmesan cheese, grated
salt and freshly ground black pepper

Heat the olive oil in a small saucepan, add the onion and garlic and fry over a moderate heat for 5 minutes. Stir in the tomatoes, with salt and pepper to taste. Bring to the boil, lower the heat and simmer for 10 minutes, to make a thick tomato sauce.

Cut courgette slices into halves or quarters, depending on size. Shake in a bag with the flour to coat evenly, and fry in the butter in a frying pan until brown on both sides.

In a shallow baking dish, layer the courgettes then half the mozzarella, then the tomato mixture and the remaining mozzarella. Sprinkle over the Parmesan. Bake in a preheated oven, 190°C (*375°F*), Gas Mark 5, for 30 minutes.

TOMATO, SPINACH & RICOTTA CASSEROLE

Serves 4-6

750 g (*1½ lb*) spinach, shredded
1 tablespoon water
25 g (*1 oz*) butter
1 onion, chopped
1 garlic clove, crushed
2 beefsteak tomatoes, skinned and sliced
375 g (*12 oz*) ricotta cheese
salt and freshly ground black pepper
2 tablespoons grated Parmesan cheese

Put the spinach in a saucepan with the water and a little salt. Cook for 2-3 minutes until soft, then drain well and place in a bowl.

Use a little of the butter to grease a casserole. Melt the remaining butter in a pan, add the onion and garlic and cook until soft. Stir into the spinach and mix well. Layer half the spinach, half the sliced tomatoes and half the ricotta cheese in the casserole. Repeat the layers, seasoning each layer with salt and pepper. Sprinkle the Parmesan over the top.

Cover casserole and bake in a preheated oven, 180°C (*350°F*), Gas Mark 4, for 30 minutes. Remove lid and return to the oven for a further 10 minutes to brown the top.

Illustrated opposite

TOMATO-STUFFED AUBERGINE

Serves 2

1 aubergine
2 tablespoons olive oil
1 garlic clove, crushed
1 small onion, chopped
250 g (*8 oz*) tomatoes, skinned and chopped
½-1 teaspoon dried oregano
2 tablespoons grated Parmesan cheese
1 tablespoon chopped fresh parsley
salt and freshly ground black pepper

Cut the aubergine in half lengthways. Scoop out and reserve the inside, leaving 1 cm (*½ inch*) of flesh in the shell. Place the aubergine shells in an oiled baking dish and brush the insides with a little of the oil. Bake in a preheated oven, 180°C (*350°F*), Gas Mark 4, for 15 minutes.

Meanwhile, chop the aubergine flesh finely. Heat the remaining oil in a frying pan, add the garlic and onion, and fry for 5 minutes until softened. Add the aubergine flesh, tomatoes and oregano with salt and pepper to taste. Stir well and simmer for 10 minutes.

Divide the tomato mixture between the aubergine shells, sprinkle with Parmesan and parsley and return to the oven for a further 15-20 minutes. Serve hot or cold.

BAKED TOMATOES WITH GARLIC

Serves 6

4 tablespoons olive oil
6 plum tomatoes, halved
1 garlic clove, finely chopped
3 tablespoons chopped fresh parsley
25 g (*1 oz*) fresh breadcrumbs
salt and freshly ground black pepper

Heat the olive oil in a large frying pan. Add the tomatoes, cut-side down and fry over a low heat for 6 minutes, turning over after 4 minutes.

Place in an ovenproof dish and sprinkle with salt and pepper to taste, the garlic, parsley and breadcrumbs. Drizzle with the oil remaining in the frying pan. Bake in a preheated oven, 180°C (*350°F*), Gas Mark 4, for 40 minutes.

RATATOUILLE

Serves 6-8

500 g (*1 lb*) aubergines
750 g (*1½ lb*) large, firm ripe
tomatoes, skinned
125 ml (*4 fl oz*) olive oil
2 large red onions, sliced
250 g (*8 oz*) green peppers, cored, seeded
and cut into 2.5 cm (*1 inch*) squares
500 g (*1 lb*) courgettes, trimmed
and cut into 2.5 cm (*1 inch*) slices
3 large garlic cloves, halved lengthways
water or tomato juice (see method)
2 teaspoons sugar
salt and freshly ground black pepper

TO GARNISH:

finely chopped fresh parsley
black olives

Trim off the stem ends of the aubergines and discard. Cut aubergines into 2.5 cm (*1 inch*) cubes. Toss in salt and leave in a colander for 30 minutes to extract the excess moisture.

Cut the tomatoes into chunks and scoop out the pulp and seeds into a sieve set over a measuring jug. Rinse the aubergine cubes under cold running water, drain and pat dry with kitchen paper.

Heat half the oil in a wide, flameproof casserole. Add the onions and simmer, stirring frequently, for 10 minutes, or until softened. Using a slotted spoon, transfer the onions to a bowl and set aside.

Add the green peppers to the oil remaining in the pan and soften them over a low heat for 5 minutes. Add them to the onions. Raise the heat to moderate, add the courgettes and fry until golden. Add them to the other fried vegetables. Add the remaining oil to the pan. When hot, fry the aubergine cubes. Return all the vegetables to the casserole, together with the chopped tomatoes and the garlic.

Rub the strained tomato pulp through the sieve and make up to 125 ml (*¼ pint*) with water or tomato juice if necessary. Stir in the sugar, 1 tablespoon of salt and a generous grinding of black pepper. Pour the mixture over the vegetables. Stir lightly, cover and cook over a low heat for 30 minutes. Turn the vegetables over from top to bottom and cook, covered, for a further 15 minutes. Most of the cooking liquid should have evaporated. If not, remove the lid and cook for a further 5-10 minutes – the vegetables should be soft but not disintegrating.

Allow the ratatouille to cool slightly before adjusting the seasoning to taste. Serve it lukewarm or lightly chilled, garnished with the finely chopped parsley and black olives.

FRENCH BEAN & TOMATO CASSEROLE

Serves 6

**750 g (*1½ lb*) French beans,
topped and tailed
250 g (*8 oz*) broccoli florets
250 g (*8 oz*) mozzarella cheese
15 g (*½ oz*) butter or margarine
2 onions, sliced
1-2 garlic cloves, sliced
625 g (*1¼ lb*) plum tomatoes, skinned,
seeded and chopped
2 spring onions, sliced
2 tablespoons grated Parmesan cheese
salt and freshly ground black pepper
a few fresh herb sprigs,
to garnish (optional)**

Bring a large saucepan of water to the boil, add the French beans and broccoli florets and blanch for 3 minutes. Drain.

Meanwhile, grate 25 g (*1 oz*) of the mozzarella and thinly slice the remainder. Set aside.

Melt the butter or margarine in a saucepan, add the sliced onions and garlic and fry gently for 5 minutes until soft. Stir in the chopped tomatoes, bring to the boil and cook, un-covered, for 15 minutes until thickened. Stir in the sliced spring onions and season to taste with salt and pepper, then add the French beans and broccoli florets.

Spoon a layer of the bean and tomato mixture into the bottom of a greased ovenproof dish. Cover with a layer of sliced mozzarella cheese, then another layer of bean and tomato mixture. Continue with these layers until all the ingredients are used up, finishing with a layer of mozzarella.

Mix the grated mozzarella and Parmesan together and sprinkle over the top of the cassserole. Bake in a preheated oven, 180°C (*350°F*), Gas Mark 4, for 30-35 minutes. Serve hot, garnished with fresh herb sprigs, if liked.

Illustrated opposite

COURGETTE & TOMATO GOUGERE

Serves 3-4

375 g (*12 oz*) courgettes, trimmed and sliced
2 tablespoons sunflower oil
2 onions, chopped
1 green pepper, cored, seeded and sliced
250 g (*8 oz*) tomatoes, skinned and quartered
1 teaspoon dried oregano
2 teaspoons grated Parmesan cheese
salt and freshly ground black pepper

CHOUX PASTRY:

65 g (*2½ oz*) wholemeal flour
pinch of salt
50 g (*2 oz*) butter
150 ml (*¼ pint*) water
2 eggs, beaten

Place the courgette slices in a colander, sprinkle with salt and set aside for 30 minutes to draw out some of the excess liquid.

Heat the sunflower oil in a large frying pan, add the chopped onions and cook over a gentle heat for 5 minutes. Stir in the green pepper. Rinse and drain the courgettes and add them to the frying pan. Cook for a further 5 minutes, stirring occasionally. Add the quartered tomatoes, oregano and seasoning to taste. Cook for about 10 minutes until beginning to soften. Set aside.

To make the choux paste, sift the flour and salt together on to a sheet of greaseproof paper, returning the bran retained in the sieve to the flour. Melt the butter in a small saucepan, add the measured water and bring to the boil. When bubbling, remove the pan from the heat and immediately add the flour all at once. Beat the mixture until it is smooth and leaves the sides of the pan clean. Allow to cool slightly, then gradually add the eggs, beating well between each addition.

Spoon the choux paste around the edge of a shallow 1.5 litre (*2½ pint*) ovenproof dish. Turn the vegetable mixture into the centre and sprinkle with the grated Parmesan.

Cook in a preheated oven, 200°C (*400°F*), Gas Mark 6, for 30-35 minutes until the choux pastry is golden brown and risen. Serve immediately with a green salad.

TOMATO RICE

Serves 4-6

50 g (*2 oz*) butter
500 g (*1 lb*) ripe tomatoes, skinned
and finely chopped
¼ teaspoon cayenne pepper
½ teaspoon sugar
1 large onion, sliced
1 tablespoon sunflower oil
1 cm (*½ inch*) piece of fresh root ginger, peeled
and finely chopped
1 garlic clove, crushed
375 g (*12 oz*) long-grain rice, washed, soaked
in cold water for 30 minutes and drained
salt and freshly ground black pepper
chopped fresh parsley, to garnish

Melt half the butter in a saucepan. Add the tomatoes, cayenne, sugar and salt. Cook, stirring occasionally, for 5 minutes. Set aside.

Gently fry onion in the oil and remaining butter in a large pan, stirring occasionally, for 3-4 minutes. Add the ginger and garlic and fry until onion is soft. Add rice, increase heat and fry, stirring, 1 minute. Pour in the tomato mixture, season, and add boiling water to cover rice by 1 cm (*½ inch*). When the liquid boils rapidly, cover, reduce heat to very low and simmer 12-15 minutes or until rice is cooked and all the liquid has been absorbed. Serve immediately, garnished with parsley.

MACARONI WITH SAUSAGE & TOMATO SAUCE

Serves 4

500 g (*1 lb*) Italian sausages, skinned
2 tablespoons olive oil
2 garlic cloves, crushed
1 onion, roughly chopped
1 red pepper, cored, seeded and cut into cubes
750 g (*1½ lb*) beefsteak tomatoes,
skinned and chopped
1 teaspoon dried oregano
2 tablespoons tomato purée
75 ml (*3 fl oz*) Marsala or sherry
250 g (*8 oz*) macaroni
25 g (*1 oz*) butter
salt and freshly ground black pepper

Break each sausage into four or five pieces. Heat oil in a saucepan and fry garlic and onion until softened and lightly coloured. Add sausage to the pan, fry until evenly browned. Add red pepper, tomatoes and oregano. Stir in tomato purée and Marsala or sherry with salt and pepper to taste. Cook gently, uncovered, for 12-15 minutes.

Cook the macaroni in plenty of salted boiling water for 8-10 minutes, or according to packet instructions, until just tender. Drain well, tip into a bowl and stir in the butter. Pour the sauce over the pasta, toss to mix, and serve.

SPAGHETTI WITH TOMATO & MUSSEL SAUCE

Serves 4

2.4 litres (*4 pints*) fresh mussels
150 ml (*¼ pint*) water
5 tablespoons olive oil
1 onion, finely chopped
2 garlic cloves, sliced
750 g (*1½ lb*) tomatoes, skinned and chopped
375 g (*12 oz*) spaghetti or vermicelli
salt and freshly ground black pepper
flat leaf parsley, to garnish

First, prepare the mussels. Put them in a bowl or sink with cold water to cover. Discard any mussels which are open or which float to the top. Scrub the mussels to remove any barnacles and remove the beards. Soak in fresh cold water until ready to cook.

Put the mussels into a large saucepan with the measured water. Heat briskly, shaking the pan occasionally, for 5-6 minutes or until the shells open. Discard any mussels that do not open. Remove from the heat and drain off the water. Reserve a few of the mussels in their shells for the garnish. Remove the rest of the mussels from their shells and set aside.

Heat 3 tablespoons of the olive oil in a large saucepan. Add the chopped onion and sauté for 5 minutes until soft. Stir in the garlic, then add the chopped tomatoes. Simmer gently for about 30 minutes until the tomatoes have reduced to a pulp.

Cook the spaghetti or vermicelli in a large saucepan of lightly salted boiling water for about 10 minutes, or according to packet instructions, until just tender. Drain the pasta thoroughly. Pour the remaining olive oil into a warm dish, add the pasta and toss until lightly coated.

Season the tomato sauce with salt and pepper to taste, add the shelled mussels and heat through, stirring. Pile the sauce on top of the pasta. Garnish with the reserved mussels and flat leaf parsley and serve immediately.

Illustrated opposite

PASTA SHELLS WITH RICH TOMATO SAUCE

Serves 3-4

**250 g (*8 oz*) wholewheat pasta shells
or spaghetti**

TOMATO SAUCE:

25 g (*1 oz*) butter
1 large onion, sliced
1 garlic clove, crushed
**750 g (*1½ lb*) ripe beefsteak tomatoes,
skinned and chopped**
2 tablespoons tomato purée
2 teaspoons caster sugar
**2 tablespoons chopped fresh marjoram,
or 2 teaspoons dried oregano**
**150 ml (*¼ pint*) vegetable stock, or half stock
and half red wine**
salt and freshly ground black pepper

CRUNCHY DRESSING:

5 g (*¼ oz*) butter
25 g (*1 oz*) sunflower seeds
25 g (*1 oz*) fresh wholemeal breadcrumbs

To make the tomato sauce, melt the butter in a large saucepan and fry the onion and crushed garlic for about 5 minutes until tender but not brown. Add the chopped tomatoes, tomato purée, caster sugar, marjoram or oregano, and stock or stock and wine. Stir in salt and pepper to taste. Half cover the pan and simmer gently for 25 minutes. Remove the lid, increase the heat and cook for 2-3 minutes more to reduce the sauce. It should have a thick, rich consistency. Keep the sauce hot.

Cook the pasta in a large pan of salted boiling water according to packet instructions, until just tender.

While the pasta is cooking, prepare the dressing. Heat the butter in a small frying pan, add the sunflower seeds and brown slightly, stirring and shaking the pan (be careful as they will jump about in the heat), then stir in the breadcrumbs. When both are brown, spoon on to a plate and set aside.

Drain the cooked pasta thoroughly and turn into a warm serving dish, spoon the hot sauce over and top with the crunchy dressing. Serve immediately.

TOMATO & AUBERGINE SOUFFLE LASAGNE

Serves 4-6

2 aubergines, about 500 g (*1 lb*), cut into
1 cm (*½ inch*) thick slices
4 tablespoons sunflower oil
2 large onions, sliced
2 garlic cloves, crushed
150 g (*5 oz*) no pre-cook spinach lasagne
(about 8 sheets)
750 g (*1½ lb*) ripe tomatoes, sliced
1 tablespoon chopped fresh basil,
or 1 teaspoon dried
150 ml (*¼ pint*) vegetable stock
salt and freshly ground black pepper

SOUFFLE TOPPING:

15 g (*½ oz*) butter
15 g (*½ oz*) plain flour
300 ml (*½ pint*) milk
2 eggs, separated

Put the aubergine slices in a colander, sprinkle with salt and set aside for 30 minutes to draw out some of the excess liquid.

Heat 1 tablespoon of the oil in a large frying pan. Fry the onions and garlic for 5 minutes until soft but not brown. Spoon into a dish and set aside.

Rinse the aubergine slices, drain, then dry with kitchen paper. Heat 2 tablespoons of the remaining oil in the pan and fry half the slices on both sides until golden brown. Drain on kitchen paper. Add the rest of the oil to the pan and fry the remaining aubergine slices.

Lightly oil a large shallow ovenproof dish. Lay four lasagne sheets in the bottom. Cover with a layer of aubergine slices, then a layer of cooked onion, then one of tomato slices. Sprinkle with salt, plenty of black pepper and half the basil. Repeat the layering once more, using all the remaining lasagne, vegetables and herbs. Pour over the stock to enable the pasta to rehydrate.

To make the soufflé topping, melt the butter in a small saucepan, stir in the flour and cook for 1 minute. Gradually add the milk, stirring until the sauce boils and thickens. Cool slightly, then stir in the egg yolks and season.

Whisk the egg whites in a grease-free bowl until stiff and fold them carefully into the sauce. Spoon the mixture into the dish, covering the top layer completely. Bake in a preheated oven, 180°C (*350°F*), Gas Mark 4, for 45 minutes until the soufflé has risen and is browned.

Serve the lasagne piping hot with granary bread to soak up the juices.

TOMATO PIZZA

Serves 1-2

200 g (*7 oz*) strong plain flour
7 g (*¼ oz*) sachet fast-action dried yeast
6 tablespoons olive oil
750 g (*1½ lb*) tomatoes, skinned and chopped
1 onion, chopped
1 teaspoon sugar
1-2 garlic cloves, chopped
2 teaspoons dried oregano
2 sun-dried tomatoes, cut into thin strips
5 tablespoons freshly grated Parmesan cheese
salt and freshly ground black pepper

For the dough, sift flour into a bowl, stir in yeast. Make a well in the centre, add 125 ml (*4 fl oz*) hand-hot water, 1 tablespoon of the oil and 1 teaspoon of salt. Mix to a soft dough, knead on lightly floured surface until smooth, about 10 minutes. Roll out to 25 cm (*10 inch*) circle. Place on a lightly floured baking sheet. Pinch a slightly thicker rim with your fingers. Cover with oiled polythene, leave to prove for 30 minutes, while preparing topping.

In a frying pan, cook the tomatoes, onion and sugar in 3 tablespoons of the oil over a low heat for 15 minutes, or until thick. Brush pizza base with a little of remaining oil, top with the sauce, then add the garlic, oregano, sun-dried tomatoes and salt and pepper. Sprinkle with cheese and remaining oil, bake in a preheated oven, 220°C (*425°F*), Gas Mark 7, for 20-25 minutes until bubbling and golden. Serve hot.

TOMATO & MOZZARELLA PIZZA

Serves 1-2

3 tablespoons olive oil
500 g (*1 lb*) tomatoes, skinned and chopped
1 home-made pizza base (see opposite)
125 g (*4 oz*) mozzarella cheese, grated
50 g (*2 oz*) pepperoni, sliced
3 large tomatoes, sliced
5 sun-dried tomatoes, halved
1 green pepper, sliced
freshly ground black pepper

Heat 2 tablespoons of the olive oil in a large frying pan. Add the chopped tomatoes and cook over a low heat for 15 minutes, or until the sauce is thick.

Place the prepared pizza base on a lightly floured baking sheet. Spread the sauce over the pizza dough. Sprinkle over half of the mozzarella. Top with the pepperoni, sliced tomatoes, sun-dried tomatoes and green pepper. Sprinkle over the remaining cheese, olive oil and black pepper.

Bake in a preheated oven, 220°C (*425°F*), Gas Mark 7, for 20-25 minutes until the pizza is bubbling and golden.

Illustrated opposite

TOMATO-STUFFED PANCAKES

Serves 4

BATTER:

125 g (*4 oz*) plain flour, sifted

¼ teaspoon salt

1 egg, beaten

300 ml (*½ pint*) milk

oil, for frying

FILLING:

25 g (*1 oz*) butter

½ onion, finely chopped

4 tomatoes, skinned and roughly chopped

125 g (*4 oz*) mushrooms, chopped

1 teaspoon mixed dried herbs

25 g (*1 oz*) fresh white breadcrumbs

salt and freshly ground black pepper

SAUCE TOPPING:

40 g (*1½ oz*) butter

40 g (*1½ oz*) plain flour

300 ml (*½ pint*) milk

75 g (*3 oz*) Cheddar cheese, grated

To make the pancake batter, sift the flour and salt together in a bowl. Make a well in the centre and add the beaten egg and half of the milk. Gradually incorporate the flour into the liquid to make a smooth batter. Stir in the rest of the milk.

Grease a 20 cm (*8 inch*) frying pan with a little of the oil. Pour in enough batter to cover the bottom of the pan, tilting the pan so that the batter covers it evenly. Cook over a moderate heat until the bottom of the pancake is golden brown, then flip or turn the pancake over and cook the other side briefly. Keep the pancake warm while making seven more pancakes in the same way.

For the filling, melt the butter and fry the chopped onions, tomatoes and mushrooms until reduced to a pulp. Stir in the herbs and breadcrumbs, and season well. Divide the filling between the pancakes and roll them up. Arrange side by side in an ovenproof dish.

To make the sauce topping, melt the butter in a heavy-based saucepan. Stir in the flour and cook for 1 minute. Gradually add the milk, stirring until the sauce boils and thickens. Simmer for 3-4 minutes, stirring.

Stir 50 g (*2 oz*) of the cheese into the white sauce, season and pour over the pancakes. Sprinkle over the remaining cheese. Bake in a preheated oven, 190°C (*375°F*), Gas Mark 5, for 20 minutes.

TOMATO & BACON FONDUE

Serves 4

1 garlic clove
125 g (*4 oz*) rindless streaky bacon
150 ml (*¼ pint*) dry white wine
2 teaspoons cornflour
2 beefsteak tomatoes, skinned
and finely chopped
175 g (*6 oz*) Cheddar cheese, grated
175 g (*6 oz*) Gruyère cheese, grated
few drops of Worcestershire sauce
pinch of mustard powder
salt and freshly ground black pepper

Cut the garlic clove in half and rub the inside of a fondue pan with the cut edge. Discard the garlic. Grill the bacon until crisp, drain on kitchen paper, and chop into bite-sized pieces.

Mix 1 tablespoon of wine with the cornflour in a small bowl, pour remaining wine into fondue pan. Add tomatoes and heat gently until hot. Gradually stir in the cheeses, beating gently. Add the cornflour mixture to the pan; stir over a moderate heat until thickened. Stir in the bacon. Add a few drops of Worcestershire sauce, a pinch of mustard powder and salt and pepper to taste.

Serve with cubes of crusty French bread, cauliflower florets and chunks of courgette to dip into the fondue.

WALNUT, CHEESE & TOMATO LOAF

Serves 4-6

250 g (*8 oz*) walnuts, ground
250 g (*8 oz*) tomatoes, skinned and thinly sliced
125 g (*4 oz*) Cheddar cheese, grated
1 onion, grated
1 tablespoon chopped fresh marjoram
or oregano
1 egg, beaten
salt and freshly ground black pepper

Combine the ground walnuts, sliced tomatoes, grated cheese and onion and chopped herbs in a bowl. Add salt and pepper to taste and stir in the beaten egg.

Spoon the mixture into a lightly greased 500 g (*1 lb*) loaf tin and press down well. Bake in a preheated oven, 200°C (*400°F*), Gas Mark 6, for 30-40 minutes, or until brown on top. Cool the loaf in the tin, turn it out on to a serving dish and serve with a salad.

TOMATO & FETA TARTS

Makes 18-20

**750 g (*1½ lb*) tomatoes, skinned,
seeded and chopped**
1 small onion, finely chopped
2 garlic cloves, chopped
2 tablespoons tomato purée
1 tablespoon chopped fresh basil
2 teaspoons chopped fresh thyme
125 g (*4 oz*) feta cheese, crumbled
12 plump black olives, pitted
**6 drained canned anchovy fillets,
split lengthways**
3 tablespoons olive oil
salt and freshly ground black pepper

PASTRY:

125 g (*4 oz*) wholemeal flour
125 g (*4 oz*) plain flour
125 g (*4 oz*) full-fat soft cheese
generous pinch of salt
3 tablespoons natural yogurt
2 egg yolks

To make the pastry, put the flours into a liquidizer or food processor with the soft cheese and blend to a fine crumb texture. Beat the salt, yogurt and egg yolks together. Add to the dry ingredients and process until the mixture forms a ball of dough, being careful not to overmix. Wrap closely and chill for 1 hour before using.

Since this pastry is more elastic than standard shortcrust pastry and is more prone to losing its shape, roll out the pastry thinly on a floured board and then leave it to relax for 10 minutes before cutting. Using a fluted pastry cutter stamp out circles from the pastry and use to line 18-20 individual patty tins; press up the edges well.

Mix the chopped tomatoes, onion, garlic, tomato purée, basil and thyme in a shallow saucepan. Add salt and pepper to taste. Simmer for about 20 minutes until the mixture is thick and pulpy.

Divide the tomato filling between the pastry cases, adding a little feta cheese to each one. Roll each black olive in a strip of anchovy fillet and place one on each tart. Dribble over a little olive oil.

Bake the tarts in a preheated oven, 190°C (*375°F*), Gas Mark 5, for 25-30 minutes until the filling is a rich red colour, and the pastry has taken on some of the colour from the filling. Serve immediately.

Illustrated opposite

TOMATO TART

Serves 4-6

750 g (*1½ lb*) ripe, firm tomatoes,
skinned and quartered
250 g (*8 oz*) frozen puff pastry, thawed
75 g (*3 oz*) Gruyère or mild
Cheddar cheese, grated
25 g (*1 oz*) butter, softened
4 tablespoons double cream
2 eggs, lightly beaten
salt and freshly ground black pepper

Squeeze tomato quarters gently over a colander to rid them of excess moisture. Chop and leave to drain in the colander.

Roll the pastry out thinly and line a 23-25 cm (*9-10 inch*) fluted tart tin with a removable base. Sprinkle pastry evenly with 25 g (*1 oz*) of the cheese. Work remaining cheese in a bowl to a fluffy paste with the butter and cream. Then beat in the eggs and season lightly.

Season tomatoes and spread evenly over the pastry base. Spoon the egg and cheese mixture over the tomatoes. Place tart on a preheated heavy baking sheet in a preheated oven, 220°C (*425°F*), Gas Mark 7. After 15 minutes, reduce heat to 180°C (*350°F*), Gas Mark 4. Bake tart for 20 minutes longer, or until filling is puffed and richly coloured and pastry is crisp and cooked through. Serve the tart as a first course or with a salad as a main course.

TOMATO & BACON TURNOVERS

Makes 4

25 g (*1 oz*) butter
1 onion, finely chopped
175 g (*6 oz*) rindless back bacon, chopped
250 g (*8 oz*) tomatoes, skinned,
seeded and chopped
1 tablespoon chopped fresh parsley
1 tablespoon tomato purée
250 g (*8 oz*) packet frozen puff pastry, thawed
salt and freshly ground black pepper
beaten egg, to glaze

Melt butter in a frying pan, add the onion and bacon and fry, stirring, for 4 minutes. Add tomatoes, parsley and tomato purée with plenty of pepper to taste. Cook, stirring, for 5 minutes or until thickened. Set aside to cool.

On a floured board, roll out pastry to a 30 cm (*12 inch*) square. Cut into four equal squares and dampen the edges with egg. Divide the bacon filling between the squares. Fold over each square diagonally to form triangle-shaped turnovers. Press edges together to seal.

Brush turnovers with beaten egg and place on a greased baking sheet. Bake in a preheated oven, 220°C (*425°F*), Gas Mark 7, for 25 minutes until golden. Cool on a wire rack.

TANDOORI CHICKEN IN TOMATO SAUCE

Serves 4

**1.5 kg (*3 lb*) chicken, skinned
and cut into 8 portions
chopped fresh parsley, to garnish**

MARINADE:

**4 tablespoons lemon juice
1 garlic clove, crushed
½ teaspoon ground coriander
½ teaspoon chilli powder
1 teaspoon garam masala
4 tablespoons natural yogurt
1 teaspoon ground cumin
1 tablespoon paprika
2.5 cm (*1 inch*) piece of fresh root ginger,
finely chopped
2 tablespoons oil
salt and freshly ground black pepper**

SAUCE:

**50 g (*2 oz*) butter
1 teaspoon salt
½ teaspoon sugar
500 g (*1 lb*) tomatoes, skinned and quartered
1 teaspoon garam masala
3 tablespoons double cream**

Make cuts all over the surface of the chicken. Mix the ingredients for the marinade in a bowl. Rub the mixture over the chicken portions until well coated. Place the chicken on a plate, cover and leave in a cool place for 4 hours, or refrigerate overnight, to marinate.

Transfer the chicken portions to a greased baking tin and baste with the oil. Cook in a preheated oven, 200°C (*400°F*), Gas Mark 6, for 30 minutes. Baste with the juices several times during cooking.

To make the sauce, melt the butter in a large frying pan and add the salt, sugar and tomatoes. Cook, uncovered, for about 15 minutes, stirring occasionally. Rub the mixture through a sieve or purée it first in a liquidizer or food processor, and then rub through a sieve. Return the tomato sauce to the rinsed pan. Add the garam masala and simmer for 10 minutes. Remove the pan from the heat and stir in the cream.

Add the cooked chicken pieces to the sauce. Heat through but do not boil. Transfer to a heated serving dish, sprinkle with the chopped parsley and serve.

CHICKEN & TOMATO CURRY

Serves 4

50 g (*2 oz*) butter
2 onions, finely chopped
2.5 cm (*1 inch*) piece of fresh ginger,
peeled and chopped
2 teaspoons garam masala
1 teaspoon ground cumin
¼ teaspoon cayenne pepper
150 ml (*¼ pint*) natural yogurt
125 g (*4 oz*) tomatoes, skinned and chopped
1.75 kg (*3½ lb*) chicken, cut into 8 portions
150 ml (*¼ pint*) chicken stock
salt

Melt the butter in a large saucepan, add the chopped onions and ginger and fry over a gentle heat until soft. Add the garam masala, cumin and cayenne pepper and cook for 2 minutes, then gradually stir in the yogurt a tablespoon at a time. Stir in the chopped tomatoes with salt to taste and cook over a low heat for a further 2-3 minutes.

Add the chicken pieces and the stock to the saucepan. Bring to the boil, cover the pan and simmer the curry for 45 minutes or until the chicken is tender. Serve with pilau rice, poppadums and sambals.

COUNTRY CHICKEN WITH PEPPERS & TOMATOES

Serves 4

1.5 kg (*3 lb*) chicken, cut into quarters,
or 4 chicken portions
seasoned flour, for dredging
4 tablespoons sunflower oil
2 onions, chopped
2 green peppers, cored, seeded and sliced
2 garlic cloves, crushed
500 g (*1 lb*) plum tomatoes, chopped
500 ml (*17 fl oz*) red wine
1 tablespoon tomato purée
175 ml (*6 fl oz*) chicken stock
1 teaspoon dried oregano
1 bay leaf
pitted black olives, to garnish

Dredge the chicken pieces in the seasoned flour in a strong polythene bag. Shake off the excess flour. Heat the oil in a large frying pan, add the onions and sauté for 3 minutes. Add the chicken and cook until golden all over.

Add all the remaining ingredients, except the black olives, to the pan. Cover and simmer gently for 40 minutes. Spoon the chicken and vegetables on to a warmed serving dish and garnish with the black olives. Serve at once.

Illustrated opposite

STEAK WITH FRESH TOMATO SAUCE

Serves 4

4 rib or rump steaks, 2 cm (*¾ inch*) thick
olive oil, for sprinkling and frying
125 ml (*4 fl oz*) dry red wine or beef stock
salt and freshly ground black pepper
parsley sprigs, to garnish

SAUCE:

2 tablespoons olive oil
3 garlic cloves, crushed
500 g (*1 lb*) plum tomatoes, skinned, seeded
and chopped
a few fresh basil leaves,
or ½ teaspoon dried oregano

Beat the steaks with a rolling pin to tenderize. Season, sprinkle with oil and leave to stand.

For the sauce, heat the oil in a saucepan, sauté the garlic for 1 minute. Add the tomatoes and season to taste. Bring to the boil then cook over a moderate heat 5 minutes, until tomatoes are just softened. Add the basil or oregano.

Oil the base of a large frying pan and sauté the steaks over a moderate heat for 2 minutes each side, until lightly browned. Add the wine or stock. Top each steak with a thick layer of the sauce, cover the pan tightly and cook over a low heat for 6-10 minutes or until the steaks are tender and cooked to your liking. Serve at once, garnished with parsley.

PORK CHOPS WITH JUNIPER BERRIES & TOMATOES

Serves 4

4 tablespoons olive oil
4 pork chops, about 250 g (*8 oz*) each
2 shallots, chopped
1 garlic clove, chopped
8 juniper berries, roughly crushed
375 g (*12 oz*) tomatoes, skinned and
roughly chopped
5 tablespoons gin or vodka
150 ml (*¼ pint*) chicken stock
½ tablespoon chopped fresh thyme,
or ½ teaspoon dried
salt and freshly ground black pepper

Heat the oil in a deep frying pan. Add pork chops, fry briskly for 3-4 minutes each side to brown, then remove and keep warm. Add the shallots to the pan, fry gently 2 minutes, then add the garlic and cook for 1 further minute.

Stir in the juniper berries and tomatoes, cook for 2-3 minutes, stirring. Then add the gin or vodka and boil rapidly over a brisk heat until reduced by half. Stir in the stock and the thyme. Seaon to taste with salt and pepper.

Return chops to pan, cover and simmer for 15-20 minutes, adding a little extra stock if necessary, until the chops are cooked through. Serve with baked potatoes and vegetables.

VEAL WITH TOMATOES

Serves 4

675 g (*1½ lb*) veal steak, about 1 cm
(*½ inch*) thick, cut into 2.5 cm (*1 inch*) strips
1 tablespoon flour, for dusting
4 tablespoons olive oil
1 large onion, finely chopped
250 g (*8 oz*) mushrooms, thinly sliced
500 g (*1 lb*) ripe tomatoes, skinned,
seeded and chopped
50 g (*2 oz*) flaked almonds
2 garlic cloves, roughly chopped
1 teaspoon ground cumin
1 tablespoon finely chopped fresh parsley
pinch of cayenne pepper
pinch of saffron
1 small fresh red chilli, seeded and roughly
chopped, or 1 small dried red chilli, seeded
and soaked in water for 5 minutes,
then drained and roughly chopped
50 ml (*2 fl oz*) water
salt and freshly ground black pepper

Season the strips of veal with salt and black
pepper and dust with a little flour.

Pour 2 tablespoons of the olive oil into a large
heavy-based frying pan and heat. Add the
finely chopped onions to the pan and cook for
2-3 minutes. Then add the sliced mushrooms
and cook for 3-4 minutes. Remove the
vegetables from the pan with a slotted spoon,
place on a plate and set aside.

Add the remaining olive oil and sauté the
strips of veal for 3 minutes each side, or until
the veal is lightly browned. Remove from the
frying pan and set aside. Add the chopped
tomatoes to the pan and simmer gently for
2-3 minutes.

Place the flaked almonds, roughly chopped
garlic, 1 teaspoon of salt, ground cumin,
chopped parsley, cayenne pepper, saffron and
chopped chilli in a liquidizer or food processor
with the water and process to a paste. Add
this to the tomato mixture in the frying pan
and simmer for 5 minutes.

Stir in the veal, mushrooms and onions and
simmer for 5 minutes until the veal is heated
through. Serve with rice or boiled potatoes.

PRAWN & TOMATO CURRY

Serves 3-4

500 g (*1 lb*) uncooked peeled tiger or
Mediterranean prawns, deveined
salt, for sprinkling
50 g (*2 oz*) butter or ghee
2 marmande tomatoes, skinned and sliced
3 onions, finely chopped
1 garlic clove, crushed
¼ teaspoon ground ginger
1 teaspoon chilli powder
2 teaspoons ground coriander
½ teaspoon ground turmeric
2 tablespoons unsweetened desiccated coconut
150 ml (*¼ pint*) water
2 teaspoons garam masala

Sprinkle the prawns lightly with salt. Heat the butter or ghee in a large frying pan, add the prawns and fry over a moderate heat for 2 minutes. Push the prawns to one side and stir in the tomatoes, onions, garlic and all the spices except the garam masala. Cook for 1 minute, then mix with the prawns and cook for 4 minutes more.

Add the coconut and measured water to the pan and simmer for 5 minutes. Sprinkle on the garam masala and cook for 1 minute. Serve with plain boiled rice and a selection of side dishes.

CHILLI PRAWNS & CHERRY TOMATOES

Serves 4

3 tablespoons sunflower oil
1 small onion, finely chopped
2.5 cm (*1 inch*) piece of fresh root ginger,
peeled and finely chopped
2 garlic cloves, crushed
1-2 fresh chillies, seeded and chopped,
or 1-2 teaspoons chilli powder
350 g (*12 oz*) uncooked peeled tiger prawns,
with tails left on
6-8 cherry tomatoes, halved
2 tablespoons tomato purée
1 tablespoon red or white wine vinegar
pinch of caster sugar
½ teaspoon salt

Heat the oil in a wok or large frying pan until hot. Add the onion, ginger, garlic and chillies or chilli powder. Stir-fry for 2-3 minutes or until softened, taking care not to let the ingredients brown.

Add the prawns, increase the heat to high and stir-fry for 1-2 minutes, or until they turn pink. Add the remaining ingredients and stir-fry for several minutes or until the mixture is thick, taking care not to let the tomatoes lose their shape. Adjust the seasoning to taste and serve at once with noodles or rice.

Illustrated opposite

MEDITERRANEAN FISH & TOMATO CASSEROLE

Serves 4

2 rashers rindless streaky bacon, chopped
1 large onion, finely chopped
1 garlic clove, crushed
1 small green pepper, cored, seeded
and finely chopped
1 tablespoon plain flour
150 ml (¼ pint) dry white wine
150 ml (¼ pint) water
2 beefsteak tomatoes, skinned,
seeded and chopped
½ teaspoon dried basil
675 g (1½ lb) monkfish or other firm white fish,
skinned and cut into large chunks
salt and freshly ground black pepper
chopped fresh parsley, to garnish

Heat bacon in a large heavy-based frying pan until fat runs. Increase heat and fry onion, garlic and green pepper for 5-6 minutes or until onion is soft.

Stir in flour, cook for 1 minute. Gradually add wine and water, stirring constantly. Add tomatoes, basil and seasoning to taste. Bring sauce to the boil, stirring until it thickens. Add the fish. Cover, reduce heat and simmer 10-15 minutes or until cooked. Serve garnished with parsley.

FRESH TUNA WITH TOMATOES

Serves 4

4 tuna steaks
flour, for dusting
3 tablespoons olive oil
1 small onion, chopped
1 garlic clove, crushed
750 g (1½ lb) marmande tomatoes,
skinned and chopped
2 tablespoons chopped fresh parsley
1 bay leaf
4 anchovy fillets, mashed
6 pitted black olives
salt and freshly ground black pepper

Season the tuna with salt and pepper and dust with flour. Heat half the oil in a large shallow frying pan. Sauté the fish quickly until golden on both sides. Carefully transfer to a plate.

Add the remaining oil to the pan. When hot, add the onion and garlic and sauté for 5 minutes until soft. Stir in the tomatoes, parsley, bay leaf and anchovies. Bring to the boil and cook for about 10 minutes, or until the mixture has reduced to a thin sauce.

Season with pepper, return the fish to the pan and simmer gently for 15 minutes, turning once. Turn off the heat, add the olives and leave for 5 minutes. Transfer to a warm serving dish and serve immediately.

TOMATO BREAD

Makes 2 loaves

4-5 sun-dried tomatoes, very finely chopped
750 g (*1½ lb*) strong flour
1 teaspoon salt
1 teaspoon sugar
25 g (*1 oz*) butter or margarine,
or 1 tablespoon olive or sunflower oil
20 g (*¾ oz*) fresh yeast,
or 7 g (*¼ oz*) sachet fast-action dried yeast

Place the sun-dried tomatoes in a small bowl. Add enough boiling water to cover and set aside for 2-3 minutes.

Sift the flour and salt into a large bowl and stir in the sugar. Rub in the fat or add the oil. If using fresh yeast, put it into a separate bowl. If using fast-action dried yeast, add it to the flour in the bowl.

Drain the sun-dried tomatoes, reserving the soaking liquid in a measuring jug. Make it up to 450 ml (*¾ pint*) with lukewarm water. The temperature of the liquid should be about 43°C (*110°F*). Cream the fresh yeast, add the liquid, top with a sprinkling of flour and leave for about 10 minutes, or until the surface is covered with bubbles. Blend with the flour. If using fast-action dried yeast, stir the liquid into the yeast and flour and blend to a dough.

Turn the dough out on to a lightly floured working surface and knead thoroughly until the dough is firm and elastic and no longer feels sticky. Knead in the chopped tomatoes.

Return the dough to the mixing bowl and cover the bowl with clingfilm. Leave in a warm place for about 1 hour or until the dough has doubled in bulk. Knock back the dough again and shape.

To make two loaves: grease and warm two 500 g (*1 lb*) loaf tins. Divide the dough in half. Press out each half to a neat rectangle, the same length and three times the width of each tin. Fold the dough to fit the tins and place in the tins with the fold underneath.

To make two bloomer loaves: form the dough into two large sausage shapes and place on lightly greased baking sheets. Make equally spaced shallow cuts along the top of each.

Cover the dough lightly and leave until nearly doubled in bulk. This takes at least 20 minutes.

Bake the loaves in a preheated oven, 220°C (*425°F*), Gas Mark 7, for about 35 minutes or until cooked. When cooked the loaves should sound hollow when rapped on the base. Turn the loaves out of the tins, if using. If the sides are not as crusty as you like, simply place on a flat baking sheet and return to the oven for a few minutes.

Illustrated on pages 2-3

TOMATO & PEPPER RELISH

*Makes about 2 kg (*4 lb*)*

1 kg (*2 lb*) ripe tomatoes, skinned and chopped
1 kg (*2 lb*) red peppers, cored, seeded and finely chopped
500 g (*1 lb*) onions, finely chopped
2 red chillies, seeded and finely chopped
450 ml (*¾ pint*) red wine vinegar
175 g (*6 oz*) soft light brown sugar
4 tablespoons mustard seeds
2 tablespoons celery seeds
1 tablespoon paprika
2 teaspoons salt
2 teaspoons pepper

Combine all the ingredients in a large saucepan. Bring to the boil over a moderate heat, then lower the heat and simmer, uncovered, for about 30 minutes until most of the liquid has evaporated and the relish is of a thick, pulpy consistency. Stir frequently as the relish thickens.

Sterilize three 500 g (*1 lb*) jars. Put the clean jars open end up on a baking sheet and place in a preheated oven, 140°C (*275°F*), Gas Mark 1, for about 10 minutes until hot.

Put the relish into the hot jars. When cool, seal with vinegar-proof covers. Label the jars and store in a cool, dry place. Refrigerate once opened.

GREEN TOMATO & APPLE CHUTNEY

*Makes about 2 kg (*4 lb*)*

500 g (*1 lb*) cooking apples, peeled, cored and roughly chopped
1 kg (*2 lb*) green or unripe tomatoes, chopped
500 g (*1 lb*) onions, chopped
2 garlic cloves, crushed
2 green chillies, seeded and chopped
1 teaspoon ground ginger
1 teaspoon salt
½ teaspoon turmeric
¼ teaspoon ground cloves
50 g (*2 oz*) sultanas
300 ml (*½ pint*) vinegar
250 g (*8 oz*) soft dark brown sugar

Combine all the ingredients in a large saucepan. Bring to the boil, stirring occasionally, then reduce heat and simmer, uncovered, for 1¼-1½ hours, until the excess liquid has evaporated and the chutney is thick. Stir occasionally to make sure that the chutney does not stick to the bottom of the pan.

Have ready warmed pots. Spoon in the hot chutney and top with waxed discs, waxed sides down. Cover with airtight lids while hot. Label and store, unopened, for at least 1 month to mature. Unopened jars may be stored for up to 6 months in a cool, dry place.

Illustrated opposite

BASIC TOMATO SAUCE

*Makes about 1 litre (*1¼ pints*)*

2 mild onions, finely chopped
3 tablespoons olive oil
4 plump garlic cloves, peeled but left whole
½ large green pepper, cored, seeded
and finely diced
1 large stick celery, finely diced
1.5 kg (*3 lb*) ripe tomatoes, skinned,
and roughly chopped
1 bay leaf
2 teaspoons dried oregano or marjoram
1 teaspoon dried basil
1 teaspoon sugar (optional)
salt and freshly ground black pepper

Gently fry the onions in the oil in a large saucepan until soft. Add whole garlic cloves, and when lightly coloured, add the pepper and celery. Fry gently, stirring occasionally, until the vegetables have softened.

Add the tomatoes and herbs, season lightly. Bring sauce slowly to simmering point, cover and cook gently, stirring occasionally and mashing the tomatoes with the back of a spoon, for 40-45 minutes, or until sauce is thick and richly flavoured. Adjust the seasoning, adding sugar if necessary. Remove and discard the garlic before serving the sauce with grilled sausages or chicken drumsticks, as a pasta sauce or as a topping for pizza.

FIVE-MINUTE TOMATO SAUCE

Serves 4-6

500 g (*1 lb*) ripe beefsteak tomatoes,
skinned and quartered
a few spring onions
2-3 basil leaves, or pinch of dried
1 teaspoon brown sugar
2 tablespoons tomato purée
salt and freshly ground black pepper

Place all the ingredients into a liquidizer or food processor and blend to a purée. Place in a saucepan and heat for a few minutes.

This thin sauce has the fresh flavour of uncooked tomatoes. It is important to use spring onions as the flavour of an ordinary onion is too harsh for this short cooking time.

TOMATO MAYONNAISE

Makes about 450 ml (¾ pint)

250 g (*8 oz*) ripe tomatoes, skinned, seeded and diced
2 teaspoons tomato purée
1 tablespoon chopped fresh basil
salt and freshly ground black pepper

MAYONNAISE:
2 egg yolks
2 teaspoons Dijon mustard
300 ml (*½ pint*) olive oil, or 150 ml (*¼ pint*)
each olive and sunflower oil
1 tablespoon white wine vinegar

To make the mayonnaise, beat the egg yolks and mustard in a bowl, and add the oil, drop by drop, beating constantly. As it starts to thicken, add oil in a steady stream, then stir in the vinegar with salt and pepper to taste. Alternatively, place the egg yolks, mustard and 1 tablespoon of the oil in a liquidizer or food processor and process for 5 seconds. Dribble the remaining oil through the feed tube with the motor running, until it is all amalgamated. Add the vinegar, with salt and pepper to taste, process for 3 seconds more.

Mix the tomatoes, tomato purée and basil in a bowl. Stir in 1 tablespoon of the mayonnaise and mix well. Fold in the remaining mayonnaise. Adjust seasoning to taste.

PISTOU

Makes about 150 ml (¼ pint)

1 large ripe tomato, cut in half horizontally
40 g (*1½*) oz chopped fresh basil
4 tablespoons pine nuts, chopped
2 garlic cloves, crushed
25 g (*1 oz*) Parmesan cheese, grated
50 ml (*2 fl oz*) olive oil

Grill the tomato until soft and quite blackened on the surface. Remove the skin, chop the flesh and set aside.

Put the chopped basil in a mortar and pound until crushed. Add the pine nuts and garlic and pound again. Add the chopped tomato. Continue to pound the mixture, adding the Parmesan until smooth.

Pour on the oil, drop by drop, as if making mayonnaise, continuing to pound constantly. The sauce should have the consistency of creamed butter. Serve with wholemeal spaghetti, tagliatelle, gnocchi, noodles, or in a minestrone-type soup.

SPICY TOMATO DIP

Serves 8

2 tablespoons sunflower oil
1 large onion, finely chopped
2 large garlic cloves, finely chopped
500 g (*1 lb*) tomatoes, quartered
2 tablespoons wine vinegar
1 tablespoon caster sugar
½ teaspoon ground ginger
cayenne pepper, to taste
½ teaspoon paprika
½ teaspoon salt

Heat the oil in a saucepan. Add the onion and garlic and cook gently, stirring occasionally, for 10 minutes. Do not let the onion brown.

Add the tomatoes, vinegar, caster sugar and ground ginger, with cayenne pepper to taste. Stir. Simmer the mixture, partially covered, for 35-40 minutes until thick and pulpy, stirring occasionally towards the end of the cooking time.

Purée the dip in a liquidizer or food processor, or rub through a sieve into a bowl. Cool.

Add the paprika and salt before storing or serving the dip. It will keep, covered, in the refrigerator for 4-5 days and is delicious served with grilled sausages.

TOMATO SAMBAL

Makes 500 g (1 lb)

3 tablespoons groundnut oil
2 garlic cloves, crushed
1 small piece of tamarind, crushed,
or 4 tablespoons lime juice
1 small onion, finely chopped
3 green or red chillies, seeded and
cut into fine strips
500g (*1 lb*) firm tomatoes, skinned and diced
1 tablespoon muscovado sugar
75 ml (*3 fl oz*) canned coconut milk
1 tablespoon tomato purée
salt

TO GARNISH:

coriander sprigs
finely chopped green chilli

Heat oil in a small frying pan or wok, add the garlic, tamarind or lime juice and onion, and stir-fry for about 1 minute. Add the chillies and diced tomatoes and stir-fry for a few minutes. Add the sugar and season with salt. Stir in the coconut milk and tomato purée.

Bring to the boil, reduce the heat and cook over a medium heat for 10-15 minutes, until the mixture is fairly dry. Allow to cool, cover and chill until required. Serve garnished with fresh coriander and green chilli. (The sambal will keep in the refrigerator for about a week.)

Illustrated opposite

THE
TOMATO
COOKBOOK

TOMATO MARMALADE

Makes about 1.5 kg (3 lb)

**1.5 kg (*3 lb*) ripe tomatoes, skinned and
coarsely chopped**
2 small oranges, thinly sliced and quartered
1 lemon, thinly sliced and halved
900 g (*1 lb 13 oz*) sugar

Remove seeds from tomatoes into a sieve over
a bowl and collect the juice. Place the
tomatoes in a large heavy-based saucepan
with the juice. Add the orange and lemon
slices to the tomatoes and simmer uncovered
for 30 minutes. Add the sugar and stir until
dissolved. Bring to the boil and boil for about
1 hour or until setting point is reached: put a
little marmalade on a very cold saucer and let
cool. As it cools, if the setting point is reached
a skin will form on the surface and will
wrinkle when the marmalade is gently pushed
with one finger. Alternatively, use a sugar
thermometer – this should register 104°C
(*220°F*) when setting point is reached.

Sterilize three 500 g (*1 lb*) jars, following the
instructions in the recipe for Tomato &
Pepper Relish on page 56.

Pour the marmalade into the hot jars. Top
with waxed discs, waxed sides down. Cover
with airtight lids when cold. Label and store
the marmalade in a cool, dry place.

CARROT & TOMATO JUICE

Makes about 600 ml (1 pint)

500 g (*1 lb*) carrots, thinly sliced
500 g (*1 lb*) tomatoes, quartered
4 tablespoons lemon juice
juice of 2 oranges
150 ml (*¼ pint*) natural yogurt
1 teaspoon sugar
few drops of Tabasco sauce

Place the carrots, tomatoes, lemon and orange
juice in a liquidizer or food processor and
work to a purée. Rub through a sieve to
remove the seeds. Stir in the sugar, Tabasco
and yogurt. Serve immediately, or chill for
1 hour first.

HOME-MADE TOMATO JUICE

A glut of tomatoes provides the perfect opportunity for a supply of delicious, fresh, concentrated juice for the winter. Cocktails, clear consommés, soups and sauces can be made at a moment's notice. Just be sure to store the jars in a dark cupboard, since strong light tends to fade the brilliant colour of the juice.

Rinse the tomatoes. Chop them up if they are large and pack them into a heavy-based saucepan. Add a sprinkling of salt and sugar, but no water. Put the pan over the lowest possible heat and cook very slowly, uncovered, stirring and mashing occasionally with a wooden spoon or pestle. When the liquid comes to simmering point, continue to cook gently until the tomatoes are quite soft. Continue simmering until some of the excess water has evaporated.

Purée the tomatoes and the juice through a vegetable mouli, discarding the seeds and skins. If the tomatoes are a very 'seedy' variety, it is wise to push them through a coarse sieve first; too many seeds puréed into the juice can give it a bitter flavour. For the same reason, a liquidizer should not be used without this preliminary sieving since it tends to do too efficient a job on skins and seeds.

Pour the juice back into the pan and let it simmer, uncovered, stirring occasionally, until it has thickened to a rich, creamy consistency.

Meanwhile, prepare glass bottling jars for the juice. Wash them, rinse out with boiling water and drain upside down on a rack, then keep warm in the oven.

Prepare a double thickness of corrugated cardboard, or use a thick cloth, to line the bottom of a preserving pan or saucepan large enough to take the jars closely side by side.

Season the concentrated tomato juice to taste with more salt, sugar and freshly ground black pepper. A leaf or two of fresh basil pushed into some of the jars will make a delightful variation. Quickly pour the hot juice into the jars as the pulp deteriorates if left exposed to the air. Seal, but not too tightly.

Arrange the jars in the pan. Pour boiling water over the jars to totally cover. Then slowly let the water come back to the boil and maintain at 100°C (*210°F*) for 15 minutes to sterilize the juice.

As soon as the jars can be handled, lift them out of the pan. Put the jars aside to rest for 2-3 minutes before securing the tops as tightly as possible.

The following day, test the seal. Remove the screwbands or clips. Lift each jar by its lid. If properly sealed the lid will stay on securely and the juice may be kept for up to 6 months. If the jar has not been sealed properly, put in the refrigerator and use within 4-5 days or re-process the juice.